THE
GOSPEL
TRUTH
ABOUT
CHILDREN'S
MINISTRY

10 FRESH KidMin
RESEARCH FINDINGS

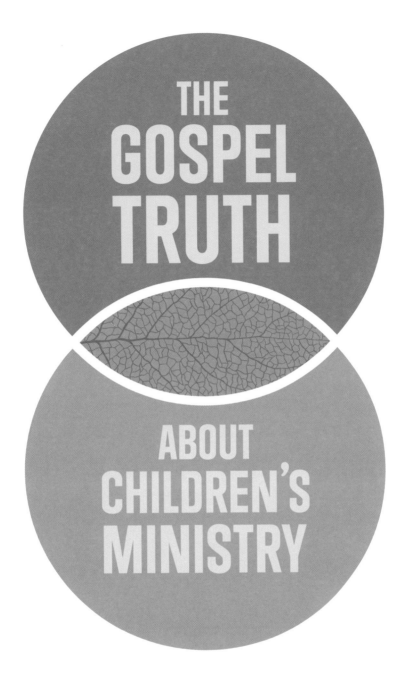

THE GOSPEL TRUTH

ABOUT CHILDREN'S MINISTRY

10 FRESH KidMin RESEARCH FINDINGS

MATT MARKINS & DAN LOVAGLIA
WITH MARK McPEAK

reach kids » equip leaders » change the world

1 East Bode Road, Streamwood, IL 60107-6658 U.S.A. • awana.org • (630) 213-2000

© 2015 Awana® Clubs International

1 2 3 4 5 6 20 19 18 17 16 15

Matt and Dan would like to thank:

Our wives Katie and Kate for their faithfulness to Christ, His Church and to us.

Our CEO, Jack Eggar, and the Global Leadership Team for your vision and wisdom.

Mark McPeak for leading our research efforts and seeking to understand the challenges that KidMin Leaders face as they minister in today's culture.

The KidMin Community who participated in the research: your voice was listened to and understood.

Senior pastors who recognize, understand, and prioritize the value of children's ministry within the mission of the church.

Mike Handler for helping us shape our thoughts and connect all the dots.

Karen Kauffman for the compelling and commanding cover design.

Nicole Bunger for the smart interior design. You made our work easy to read and understand as well as visually engaging.

The production group at Awana® for your special care and attention to detail.

And our Lord and Savior Jesus Christ for the gift of grace through You alone, and Your community, the Church.

CONTENTS

11 INTRODUCTION

19 THE PROBLEM

25 10 FRESH KɪᴅMɪɴ RESEARCH FINDINGS

Finding 1: Whatever You Do, Remember It's Still All About the Word of God. 27

Finding 2: Lifelong Discipleship Is the Outcome for Which We're Looking. 31

Finding 3: The Starting Point in Discipleship Is the Gospel:
Leading Kids to Know Christ. 35

Finding 4: Emphasis on Evangelism and the Centrality of the Bible
Is How We Make Lifelong Disciples. 39

Finding 5: It Really Does Take a Village:
Discipleship Is Relational and Engages the Family. 43

Finding 6: We're Struggling to Develop Kids Who Can Navigate Culture
and Live Out a Gospel-Centered Faith. 47

Finding 7: Children's Ministry Leaders Are Afraid We May Have Sacrificed
Substance for Fun and Entertainment. 51

Finding 8: We Need a Program That Can Meet Digital Natives Where They Are. 55

Finding 9: We Need Flexibility So We Can Customize to Our Purpose and Needs. 59

Finding 10: Children's Ministry Leaders Are Ready to Change If Curriculum Providers
Can Serve Them With the Right Resource to Help. 63

67 SUGGESTED SOLUTIONS

Suggested Solution 1: The GREAT Life Curriculum 69

Suggested Solution 2: Flexible Awana Club 73

Suggested Solution 3: Mozo Technology 77

81 APPENDIX

WE HUNDREDS
ASKED

OF CHILDREN'S MINISTRY LEADERS AND DECISION MAKERS...

"So, why did you become involved in ministering to kids?"

"How about impact ... are you seeing the results you hoped to see?"

"How's it going ... ministering to the kids?"

INTRODUCTION

We Listened to Children's Ministry Leaders and What They Said May Change Everything.

We asked hundreds of children's ministry leaders and decision makers ...

- "So, why did you become involved in ministering to kids?"

- "How about impact ... are you seeing the results you hoped to see?"

- "How's it going ... ministering to the kids?"

These seemingly simple questions, ordinary conversation-starters really, have arisen as a vitally important catalyst. Sometimes it's timing that turns something ordinary into something powerful. Asking these and other questions revealed that now is a critical and even pivotal time in children's ministry. We feel as though we're at a crossroads on the journey of ministering to children and teens and we'll need to make some critical decisions. The responses to these questions and what we all choose to do with them, might ultimately change **the entire children's ministry landscape**.

This is a bold assertion, but one made with confidence. It's reasonable, first of all, because we asked these questions (and many more related ones) in a careful and complex way through extensive research. The research was conducted with decision makers and ministers in the evangelical children's ministry community. And, even more importantly, we make this declaration with confidence because of the responses these leaders gave.

Overall, an unsettling reality was expressed by many leaders who hinted at a major disconnect between what's happening on their watch and the reasons they became involved in the first place. It's as though many people started out with a great passion to reach kids – to change the world through discipling children and teens. But now, as they look honestly at what's happening, they're disillusioned. This is seen as they talk about:

- The **priorities** in children's ministry programming.

- The **impact** of ministry efforts and activities.

- And, most importantly, the **outcomes** they're seeing in the kids and their homes.

> Overall, an unsettling reality was expressed by many leaders who hinted at a major disconnect between what's happening and the reasons they became involved in the first place.

We asked these influencers to take a step back and look at the effectiveness of their church programming, the vitality of partnership with those in the home, and above all the hearts and minds of the kids they're intending to reach.

Jesus Started the Children's Ministry Movement.

Good news: there's still great passion out there among the special people who minister with children and teens. Adults who avoid ministering to younger people often do so because they find it frustrating. But people with a calling and passion for children's ministry see it as an eternal investment. They believe they are serving God, desiring to build the next generation of believers who will be Christ to the world and continue the process of spreading His

Gospel. Perhaps it goes without saying, but they are passionate about the future of our faith and they see that the evangelism and discipleship of children and youth is of vital importance. They know a certain amount of patience is involved and that they must be willing to wait for the ultimate fruit of their efforts. The frustration of those who don't have the patience for children's ministry or who don't "get it," goes back to the beginning.

> Jesus elevated the status of children. He changed everything.

Now they were bringing even infants to Him that He might touch them. And when the disciples saw it, they rebuked them. But Jesus called them to Him, saying, "Let the children come to Me, and do not hinder them, for to such belongs the kingdom of God. Truly, I say to you, whoever does not receive the kingdom of God like a child shall not enter it." (Luke 18:15-17)

Many people who love children's ministry have been moved by this scene so intentionally included in the story of Jesus. The Gospel writers were impacted by this moment and the Holy Spirit brought it back to their memories as they wrote their accounts of our Lord's life. Jesus taught so much by what He did (and said) in this encounter. In a cultural context where children were not welcome in the seriousness of adult moments – Jesus elevated the status of children. He changed everything.

The frustrated people who didn't get it, were trying their best to keep the kids away from Jesus. After all, He was doing really "important work" (from their perspective) ministering to adults. But Jesus saw things differently. We know Jesus did not waste any opportunities to instruct and share truth as He was doing the will of His Father. This occasion was no different. Jesus clearly meant to make a bold statement in this scene under the tree (or wherever it was). He welcomed these children, blessing them in that moment and by doing so, He placed children and ministry to them into an eternal perspective.

We can rightly say that Jesus was the founder of children's ministry. He is the one who gave children their standing in the kingdom, and from a practical standpoint, in the church. He said *"let the children come to Me."* He used them as the example of faith calling us to receive His message like a child, with the faith of a child. Faithful workers worldwide have been bringing children to Jesus ever since that moment.

We can rightly say that Jesus was the founder of children's ministry.

We've Come a Long Way Since Jesus Blessed Kids Ministry.

We're in agreement that there is a strong biblical foundation found in this small incident in the Gospels and throughout the Scriptures for what children's ministry leaders and workers do. We're long past arguments over the value of ministering to our children – in our homes and in our churches. Obviously there are questions and differences of opinion about exactly *how* to go about it. However, among Bible-believing Christians the question of reaching children and bringing them to Jesus has definitely been settled. There is a growing awareness that people between the ages of 4-14 are most open to the Gospel. This is good news!

Not only has this question of ministering to children been resolved, but this category of ministry has grown immensely. The commitment to reach kids has expanded exponentially, and it is exceedingly difficult to find a church in the United States, as well as in other parts of the world, without some type of children's ministry.

Many churches have invested significantly in resources like buildings and dedicated physical spaces (some as impressive as theme parks) to reach families and kids. There are ministry professionals in this category, well-trained in higher educational contexts like seminaries, leading many trained and equipped volunteers. An entire children's ministry "industry" has arisen to help provide what churches need in terms of materials and curriculum, training and support, and many other resources.

Are We Accomplishing His Calling and Purpose in Children's Ministry?

So, with all this development and specialty, things ought to be great in children's ministry. With all the dedicated resources, all the available training, all the ministry organizations and companies offering their services, we ought to be seeing unprecedented success. At this moment in the history of the church, we ought to be fulfilling the purpose of children's ministry as never before. Right?

> The desire to lead kids to Christ and disciple them is still the purpose that burns in the hearts of those who love the Lord and who want to bring children to Him.

As part of examining the question – **Are we accomplishing what we're called to do in children's ministry?** – we must think a little more deeply about that scene with Jesus and the little children. We must ask ourselves what was Jesus really instructing us to do. After all, we believe in children's ministry and have invested heavily in carrying it out. We have complex spaces, programs, and ongoing activities. Many have dedicated their lives to this purpose.

Thinking carefully we realize these instructions are not unlike those Jesus gave at the end of His ministry in what we call the Great Commission. He commanded us to take His message to the ends of the earth and in doing so He asked us to bring everyone to Him – not just children. So Jesus is asking us to fulfill the Great Commission (*"Go therefore and make disciples …"*) with people of all ages – adult and child alike.

"Let the children come to Me …" To be consistent with what Jesus clearly instructed us to do,

He must be challenging us to go and make disciples of children. And this is the reason so many people chose children's ministry in the first place. As you'll see in the pages that follow, the desire to lead kids to Christ and disciple them is still the purpose that burns in the hearts of those who love the Lord and who want to bring children to Him. Two of the hundreds of children's ministry leaders we interviewed expressed it in their own words, this way:

> *"The objective of any children's ministry should be to equip children with the tools they will need for life to grow as a disciple, defend their faith effectively, and make other disciples along their journey."*

> *"... Christ commanded us to go and make disciples. Kids are our disciples, and our goal is to make them into future disciple makers."*

(Both comments are word-for-word responses of children's ministry decision makers to the question: "Thinking about what children's ministry in a church should accomplish, what would you say is the most important purpose or objective of children's ministry in a church?")

Maybe It's Time for Some Changes.

Despite our compelling calling in children's ministry, there is widespread concern that we've moved away from this ultimate purpose and missed the point. In the current context of unprecedented cultural change and technological advancement and in all the sophistication that has developed in the children's ministry marketplace, some important questions must be answered:

- Has the culture overwhelmed us?
- Have all the changes, innovations, and new resources made us more effective?
- Are we producing the product (kids who are committed disciples) Jesus called us to produce?

But the sum of what we heard is a concern that we may have drifted from our purpose.

We listened. We wanted to hear what our brothers and sisters in children's ministry had to say about these questions. And we heard a lot! Some of what we heard will not be surprising to those who love children's ministry. Some things may be new. But the sum of what we heard is a concern that we may have drifted from our purpose. There is a renewed desire to realign ourselves and our priorities to get back to the real reason we started ministering to kids in the first place.

Many fear that in the overwhelming busyness of running a children's ministry program, we may have lost sight of the priority — making disciples of kids, parents, and leaders.

As you read the feedback from the children's ministry community, you are likely to sense (even resonate with) what we heard. There is a willingness to change as never before. Because churches tend to be later adapters and we like to keep things the way they are, we are often slow to make changes – especially major ones. Yet, in the context of asking these core questions about the purpose of children's ministry, the current challenges churches are facing, and the results they're producing; we found an unprecedented willingness to make changes.

As we've listened we hear one sentiment expressed again and again. Many fear that in the overwhelming busyness of running a children's ministry program, we may have lost sight of the priority – making disciples of kids, parents, and leaders. And, maybe it's time we rethink and make some big decisions to get back to what we're really supposed to be all about. The words of another children's ministry leader we interviewed represent the hearts of many:

"Helping workers understand that the goal is evangelism and discipleship and relationships with families – that we aren't just running programs so kids will be busy at church."

(Word-for-word response of a children's ministry decision maker to the question: "What would you say is/are the greatest challenge(s) you face as you and your team work to successfully fulfill the purpose of your children's ministry?")

We Prepared This Work to Help

The purpose of this work *The Gospel Truth About Children's Ministry* is to give a voice to the children's ministry community. We went to great efforts to ask the questions and then to listen (through carefully planned and statistically-valid research). By listening, we learned some important things about where we are and the ways we may have gotten off track. For those who love kids and want to see them come to know, love, and serve the Savior, this content can be very helpful. In these pages, we take an honest look at where these leaders and workers say we are. We propose some timely and responsive solutions to help get us on an effective and proven trajectory to reach more kids with the Gospel and engage them in lifelong discipleship.

The purpose of this work *The Gospel Truth About Children's Ministry* is to give a voice to the children's ministry community.

THE PROBLEM

Help ...
I'm Overwhelmed!

"Things are changing so fast, no one seems able to keep up!" Amy, a seasoned children's ministry leader and mother of three continued, *"It reminds me of days at the beach when our kids were small. They loved the ocean but sometimes the waves came in so fast they'd be upended by one and they couldn't get back on their feet quickly enough to resist the next one. They loved the ocean and even the waves. But the relentlessness – not just the power – of the swells was just too much. A single wave – even a powerful one – would have been survivable; but they just kept coming and coming."*

We all feel the pressure to keep up for the sake of kids and families.

Without a rescue from Mom and Dad, the small child would be overcome by such surf. This picture resonates with Amy and with many who are ministering to and leading kids and teens.

"That's kind of how many of us feel these days. Workers, parents, and even professional children's staff all need help. We're just overwhelmed. We need something; maybe something new and innovative, something custom-made for this current craziness."

It's clear to all of us that things are rapidly changing in our churches and culture. We all feel the pressure to keep up for the sake of kids and families. **But a closer look is showing us that our programming and discipleship models might not be effective enough to stem the tides.**

At Awana We're Listening and We Want to Help.

At Awana we've worked at keeping our finger on the pulse of the church, especially in the areas of children's and youth ministries. Our calling to help churches and families develop lifelong disciples of Christ through the power of the Gospel drives us to listen. We're continually investigating and exploring to discover the truth of what's happening in the world around us. We're constantly asking God to help us discover new ideas and innovations. All of this effort is so that we can provide the help that people like Amy, and the families being served, really need.

In 2013 and again in 2014, Awana commissioned extensive primary research projects in the children's ministry world and marketplace. Why? Was it just marketing activity? Were we just looking for ways to respond and react to changes and shifts? While it's true that we wanted to keep our finger on the pulse of what's happening in ministry, our deepest desire was (and is) to serve churches so kids will come to know, love, and serve Christ for life.

The truth is our culture is changing — rapidly. Families are changing — dramatically. The kids and teens in our churches are so different; their worlds and worldviews are changing faster than ever. In response, children's ministry leaders and workers are scrambling to be effective. So, to better serve those on the frontlines, we want to understand what's going on — from all perspectives. For the sake of the Gospel, we've become students of our culture and stewards of the ministry that Christ has entrusted to us. That's why we commissioned these two recent research projects.

We never want to become complacent. **We know things change and we know organizations (even ministries) have life cycles.** We understand the bell curve of growth, plateau, and decline. But what we do in ministry partnership together is too important to stop growing and improving. We believe God has worked throughout these years to raise up, equip, and bless the ministry effectiveness and reach of Awana in local churches. To our surprise and God's glory, the results have been amazing — world changing.

The truth is
our culture is changing — rapidly.
Families are changing — dramatically.

For the faith of this and future generations, we are holding fast to our commitment to be excellent, to honor God, and to impact as many young lives and families as we can!

Comprehensive Research – What's Happening Out There?

In 2013, Awana conducted a comprehensive online survey among children's ministry leaders from across the U.S.A. Our purpose was to listen so we could really understand the issues below the waterline. We believe the people who serve children and families in and through the church day in and day out are our best source of intelligence. And we see it as our calling to do all we can to respond to what is needed with timely support and relevant resources.

Because the issues we sought to research were complex, so was our approach. We questioned multiple audiences and used a variety of methodologies. Where it was important to answer questions pertaining to the broader field of children's ministry, we used quantitative research to yield statistically reliable results. We wanted to know the numbers behind how the spectrum of children's ministry leaders describe, think, and feel about our current situation.

Where we needed deeper and more detailed insights, we conducted qualitative studies using in-depth interviews and dynamic online focus groups. The results from these activities often helped us better understand the phenomena we had quantified – answering the question "Why?" And sometimes these approaches caused us to ask follow-up questions that prompted further investigation.

We intentionally talked with children's ministry leaders who use Awana programs and those who do not use curriculum or programs offered by Awana. We surveyed across the nation and across the spectrum of region, denomination, church size, ministry approach, and so on. Our desire was to learn all we could from as many people engaged in children's ministry who were willing to share their experience and current realities with us. We wanted to be as clear as possible about what these respondents are facing as they work toward seeing the next generation transformed by the Gospel.

New Ideas and a Renewed Approach to Discipling Children – Informed by What We Learned.

We took all the ideas we gathered in the first phase of the research (2013 study) and prayerfully went to work asking God to provide us with direction, creativity, and fresh perspective. The Awana team worked with some of the most creative minds we could find to develop new ways to address the problems and challenges we discovered in our investigations. Our prayer was that a new and groundbreaking way forward would emerge through this process.

The results are inspiring! At Awana, we were thrilled with the insights and ideas resulting from the concentrated and collective efforts. With our heart still focused where it has always been – fixed on shaping disciples who can impact their generation and change the world for Christ – we developed an innovative and forward-looking approach to do exactly this.

Follow-up Research to Validate Our Ideas – Were We on Point?

In the spring of 2014, we went back to children's ministry leaders to test the concepts in another major research project. This time we tested and scrutinized the concepts and basic components of a renewed approach to discipling children (based on but not limited to the ideas learned from our initial research). For this project, we chose a combined methodology that began with a quantitative online survey that generated an impressive response – more than 850 completed surveys. This highly statistically-valid assessment (see sample validity table) of the perceptions, attitudes, and opinions of these leaders was followed by three (3) online focus groups.

Sample Validity for Quantitative Research with Children's Ministry Leaders

Records from national database and Awana database of children's ministry decision makers make up the population representing the children's ministry leaders' universe.*

858

COMPLETED SURVEYS
(SAMPLE SIZE)

±3.35%

MARGIN OF ERROR

95%

CONFIDENCE LEVEL

50/50 ASSUMED RESPONSE DISTRIBUTION

* Estimated to be 300,000 evangelical churches in the United States.

The dual methodology was used because it was important to fully vet the ideas that would serve as the basis for altering our approach to discipling children. The quantitative survey would provide statistically reliable ratings of the basic ideas and strategies that are foundational to pursuing development of a new ministry model. We can say with confidence how a representative sample of children's ministry leaders across the country feel about these ideas. We can answer the questions: Do respondents confirm or disconfirm our direction? Do they agree or disagree that we're on the right track with the solutions we're in the process of developing?

The value of following the quantification with a qualitative study is that we can begin to develop more insight about these ideas and why leaders feel as they do. Over a three-day period, the online focus group participants wrestled with the concepts in much more depth. Facilitating an environment of more open discussion, probing, and follow-up adds so much insight to the raw numbers. It enabled us to walk away with a better understanding of the why behind the ratings.

The following sections stood out to us as **the top 10 most remarkable and revealing findings** from our research. More than a thousand children's ministry leaders and decision makers have spoken: let's explore the findings.

IMPORTANT:

When establishing the validity of the research (margin of error, etc.), the reported number includes only "completed" interviews:

- Children's Ministry Marketplace Survey (2013) – 376 completes
- Children's Ministry Marketplace Survey #2 (2014) – 858 completes

For both projects, some respondents who began the survey did not complete it. The decision was made to include the responses of these "incompletes" (for the questions they answered) in the reporting. Because of this, for some questions, there are more responses than the total number of "completes" reported for the research.

For example: On page 30, 954 total respondents answered the question, but only 858 (sample size) respondents **completed** the full survey.

10 FRESH KidMin RESEARCH FINDINGS

YOU GOT INTO MINISTRY BECAUSE YOU WANTED TO REACH KIDS WITH THE GOSPEL AND ENGAGE THEM AS GROWING DISCIPLES.

1

Whatever You Do, Remember It's Still
All About the Word of God.

Whatever You Do, Remember It's Still All About the Word of God.

At a time when it feels like the ground is shifting beneath us, some things never change. The Bible continues to be the foundation children's ministry leaders want to build on.

It's clear that children's ministry leaders believe
helping kids understand and know the Bible
is the primary way of introducing kids to Jesus
and helping them walk in relationship with Him for a lifetime.

Bible-Based Program: Importance

Importance of Bible teaching as part of the program

Total Respondents: 390

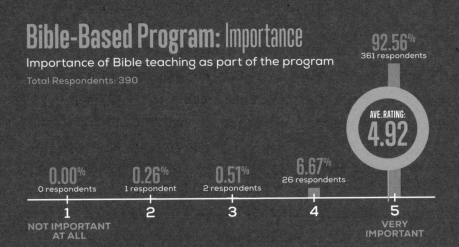

92.56%
361 respondents

AVE. RATING:
4.92

0.00%
0 respondents

0.26%
1 respondent

0.51%
2 respondents

6.67%
26 respondents

1
NOT IMPORTANT
AT ALL

2

3

4

5
VERY
IMPORTANT

In our 2013 investigation, we presented a list of 16 components that might be part of a children's ministry program or curriculum. When respondents were asked to rate the importance of each, Bible teaching was the most highly rated. In fact, on a 5-point importance scale, the average (mean) score was 4.92; this indicates nearly every respondent rated Bible teaching as a 5 (very important)! It's clear that children's ministry leaders believe helping kids understand and know the Bible is the primary way of introducing kids to Jesus and helping them walk in relationship with Him for a lifetime.

As further validation of this idea, we also asked an open-ended question on the first quantitative survey (2013): What is the single most important decision-making factor when you are considering using a children's program or materials for your church? Respondents could openly say whatever came to mind. It was an opportunity for venting or for complaining or proposing the latest trend or method. **Poised with permission to share from the heart, the most mentioned purpose for children's ministry (by 40% of respondents) was "make sure the program/materials/ministry are Bible-based."**

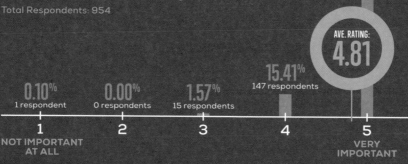

Love for the Bible: Importance

Importance of helping children develop
a love for studying and knowing the Bible

Total Respondents: 954

82.91%
791 respondents

AVE. RATING:
4.81

0.10%
1 respondent

0.00%
0 respondents

1.57%
15 respondents

15.41%
147 respondents

1   2   3   4   5

NOT IMPORTANT
AT ALL

VERY
IMPORTANT

In a different way, the 2014 research project also validated this same concept. An important focus for the quantitative study was the concept of ministry purpose — we wanted to understand what success looked like for children's ministry activities. So respondents were asked to rate 10 distinct potential ministry purposes — they were asked, "How important do you think each of these ministry purposes is?" Once again, they value the Bible above and beyond every other purpose for children's ministry. The statement "Helping children develop a love for studying and knowing the Bible" was the most highly-rated purpose (4.81 average score on a 5-point scale), 98.32% rated this purpose as important or very important (4+5 on a 5-point scale).

In Summary

First and foremost, the Bible must be the foundation of children's ministry. If our children are going to be able to withstand the surges and waves of cultural change, they must be grounded in God's Word so they can walk in a relationship with Christ as Savior, Lord, and King!

Questions for Children's Ministry Leaders and Volunteers:

1. How satisfied are you with your current ministry trajectory as it relates to developing a solid biblical foundation in the lives of kids?

2. Does your current curriculum simply leverage the Bible to teach virtues and good values? OR, does your curriculum (i.e., ministry programs) lay a strong biblical foundation that captures the redemptive story of Christ from Genesis to Revelation?

3. In your program or curriculum which comes as a first priority, Scripture/substance or subject/style?

2

Lifelong Discipleship
Is the Outcome for Which We're Looking.

Lifelong Discipleship Is the Outcome for Which We're Looking.

And Jesus came and said to them, "All authority in heaven and on earth has been given to Me. Go therefore and make disciples ..." (Matthew 28:18-19). Although it seems like innovations and changes in ministry styles have created great diversity and in some cases disparity, there is surprising focus and agreement on what the outcome of children's ministry should be. The Bible must be the basis and foundation of ministry to kids. The trajectory of developing a love for studying and knowing the Bible is an ongoing lifelong *discipleship relationship with Christ*. Helping children become forever followers of Jesus is the aim of the Great Commission — and it is the outcome of effective and appropriately-focused children's ministry. This is what a majority of children's ministry leaders told us.

A majority of children's ministry leaders told us
helping children become lifelong followers of Jesus
is the aim of the Great Commission.

Making Disciples: Importance

Importance of producing children
who are committed disciples

Total Respondents: 954

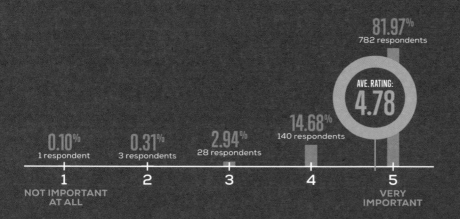

81.97%
782 respondents

AVE. RATING:
4.78

14.68%
140 respondents

0.10%
1 respondent

0.31%
3 respondents

2.94%
28 respondents

1
NOT IMPORTANT
AT ALL

2

3

4

5
VERY
IMPORTANT

It's clear from their ratings that discipleship is a top priority when it comes to the purpose of any children's ministry programming or model. In the 2014 survey, the purpose statement "Producing children who are committed disciples" is rated as important or very important (4+5 on a 5-point scale) by 96.65% of children's ministry leaders. Only Bible focus is seen as a higher purpose.

Making Disciples: Performance

Performance of producing children
who are committed disciples

Total Respondents: 936

AVE. RATING:
3.48

38.14%
357 respondents

35.04%
328 respondents

12.07%
113 respondents

13.57%
127 respondents

1.18%
11 respondents

1
NOT FULFILLING
AT ALL

2

3

4

5
FULFILLING
COMPLETELY

While discipleship is clearly a top priority as a ministry purpose, these leaders let us know that they're not doing this as well as they'd like to. Fewer than one-half (48.61%) say their church's children's ministry is fulfilling or completely fulfilling this objective (4+5 on the 5-point scale). **The disconnect between how much they value this area and how poorly they are performing is a cry for help.**

For lifelong discipleship to take root, children's ministry can't do it alone. *"We need to engage the parents in this process."* This is, in part, the cry for help. Parents don't always see the importance and value of their kids' spiritual development and they tend to be even less actively involved in the process. Some representative comments from the research bear this out.

"It is difficult to get our parents to truly understand the importance they play in their child's spiritual development."

(Qualitative response to:
Real world challenges and difficulties
to achieving ideal outcomes)

"Families are hit or miss on attendance and do not see the value of teaching their kids about Christ and what it means to have faith."

(Qualitative response to:
Real world challenges and difficulties
to achieving ideal outcomes)

In Summary

Whatever you do, don't forget the end game is a kid who grows to become a lifelong follower of Jesus Christ. Recognize that many children's ministry leaders and programs are struggling to achieve this objective. What this world needs to withstand and to overcome the waves of change is homes, churches, and children's ministries producing more and more committed disciples.

Questions for Children's Ministry Leaders and Volunteers:

1. Would you say that your children's ministry is producing disciples? How well?

2. How would you know if you were doing well or not doing so well at disciple making?

3. Does your team measure any key indicators or track Gospel growth (fruit) in the lives of kids?

4. Do you think your curriculum is helping you cultivate young disciples?

5. How do you engage parents or others at home in disciple-making?

3

The Starting Point in Discipleship Is the Gospel:
Leading Kids to Know Christ.

The Starting Point in Discipleship Is the Gospel: Leading Kids to Know Christ.

One thing was communicated with clarity – you can't forget about evangelism. Sharing the Gospel with children and challenging them to know and follow Jesus as their Lord and Savior is the essential starting point. When we asked an open-ended question about the most important purpose of children's ministry in a church of 850+ children's leaders, the most often mentioned concept was the idea of evangelizing kids. Evangelism was mentioned (unaided – without any prompting) by half (50.72%) of the respondents.

If we're going to be homes and churches that produce
these lifelong followers of the Savior,
we must be evangelizers of the Gospel of Christ.

Top 3 Answers to the Question:

Thinking about what children's ministry in a church should accomplish,

what would you say is the most important purpose or objective of children's ministry in a church?

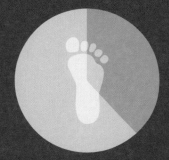

1. EVANGELIZE

Share the Gospel with/lead children
Children know God/Jesus

50.72%*

492 of 970 respondents

2. DISCIPLE

Make disciples/daily/lifelong
followers of Christ/God
Walk in relationship with Jesus

38.25%

371 of 970 respondents

3. TEACH

Teaching the Bible/doctrine
Learn/Know & Love the Word

33.30%

323 of 970 respondents

---

* Percentage of total respondents (970). When combined, chart percentages exceed 100% due to multiple answers allowed per respondent.

In the first discovery (2013 research) the importance of evangelism was validated. In the importance ratings where the Bible-centered ministry was the top characteristic when considering a children's ministry program, Gospel-centered teaching and lessons was nearly as important to respondents. This component was rated as important or very important by most leaders (mean 4.78 on 5-point scale).

In Summary

Only those who respond to the Gospel can grow to become like Jesus. If we're going to be homes and churches that produce these lifelong followers of the Savior, we must be evangelizers of the Gospel of Christ. Any program or ministry resource that is going to produce the salt and light needed to address the problems and challenges in our current world needs a strong emphasis on evangelism as part of its approach to discipleship.

Questions for Children's Ministry Leaders and Volunteers:

1. Does your children's ministry communicate the Gospel with clarity and urgency? How? When? Where?

2. Since we know it's only the Gospel that saves and transforms kids lives (not simply virtues and good values), does your curriculum align with what you know to be true?

3. Are your leaders adequately trained in understanding the Gospel as well as how to present the Gospel to others?

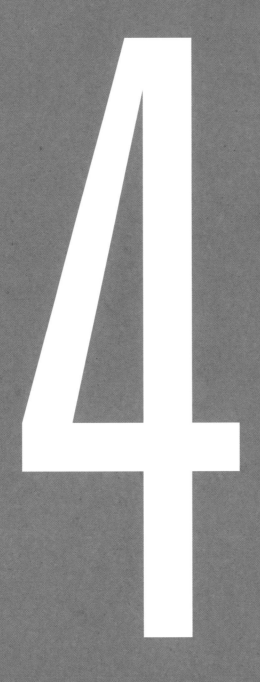

4

Emphasis on Evangelism and the Centrality of the Bible Is How We Make Lifelong Disciples.

Emphasis on Evangelism and the Centrality of the Bible Is How We Make Lifelong Disciples.

Build These Critical Components Into Your Process.

We learned that it's challenging to distinguish the components of following Christ because there is some overlap and they are all part of a complex process. We see this particularly when leaders are describing, in their own words, the most important purpose of children's ministry. Notice in the chart (on page 37) of the top three ideas mentioned (evangelize, disciple, teach) the number (count) of responses is nearly 1,200 mentions from 850+ respondents. This is true because multiple mentions were allowed and many gave a description that included several of these concepts. Rarely were these ideas simple and discreet. When summarizing (coding) responses into categories for reporting — many were classified into multiple codes.

The Bible must become the life-giving source
of truth and instruction.
All of this happens in the context of relationship.

The Most Important Purpose of Children's Ministry

PURPOSE/OBJECTIVE OF CHILDREN'S MINISTRY
Producing children who know Christ and His Word and who follow Him all their lives.

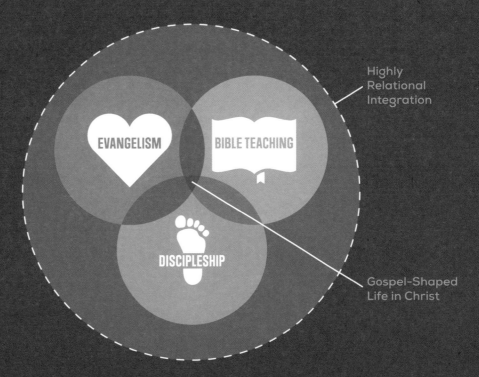

EVANGELISM

BIBLE TEACHING

DISCIPLESHIP

Highly Relational Integration

Gospel-Shaped Life in Christ

In Summary

So maybe it's complex — at least interconnected. And, maybe we all know this. It's not simply being converted (evangelized), it's more. The Bible must become the life-giving source of truth and instruction. All of this happens in the context of relationship. We follow Jesus because we know Him and we love Him. Any new ministry resource or product should appreciate this complexity and include these vital components.

Questions for Children's Ministry Leaders and Volunteers:

1. Discipleship is messier than it is linear. Does your curriculum leverage these important components (discipleship, evangelism, and Bible teaching) while leaving space for real relationships (life-on-life interactions between disciples)?

2. What role, if any, did evangelism, discipleship, and Bible teaching have on you as a child? As an adult?

3. How has discipleship impacted your family and your home?

4. Without a strong emphasis on evangelism and Bible teaching, how would you describe your ministry in five years? What needs to change as a priority today?

5. Discipleship comes at a cost. What have you invested in or eliminated to ensure discipleship of kids, families, and leaders matters in your ministry?

5

It Really Does Take a Village:
Discipleship Is Relational and Engages the Family.

It Really Does Take a Village: Discipleship Is Relational and Engages the Family.

For the leaders we researched, discipleship is a relational, side-by-side partnering process. The idea that a church or children's ministry can do it all alone is completely absent from the findings. You can almost hear leaders pleading, *"We need each other!"*

———————————— ◆ ————————————

"We can plan all we want, but if we can't awaken the parents to the importance of partnering with us to teach their child, it won't get very far."

Partnering with Parents/Caregivers: Importance

Importance of developing a partnership
with parents/caregivers to help them
in discipleship of their kids

Total Respondents: 952

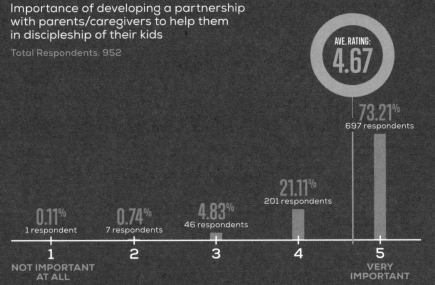

AVE. RATING:
4.67

73.21%
697 respondents

21.11%
201 respondents

0.11%
1 respondent

0.74%
7 respondents

4.83%
46 respondents

1 — NOT IMPORTANT AT ALL
2
3
4
5 — VERY IMPORTANT

Almost all of the leaders
surveyed believe
developing a partnership
with parents to disciple
their kids is one of the most
important purposes of a
children's ministry (94.32%
say it is important/very
important 4+5).

Partnering with Parents/Caregivers: Performance

Performance of developing a partnership with parents/caregivers
to help them in discipleship of their kids

Total Respondents: 939

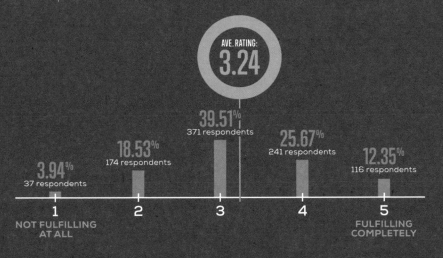

AVE. RATING:
3.24

39.51%
371 respondents

18.53%
174 respondents

25.67%
241 respondents

12.35%
116 respondents

3.94%
37 respondents

1 — NOT FULFILLING AT ALL
2
3
4
5 — FULFILLING COMPLETELY

As important as they
believe it is to partner
with parents, they report
they're not doing it very
well. Only 38.02% say
they are effectively or
very effectively fulfilling
this purpose (4+5). Of
the 10 ministry purposes
rated, this one leaders say
they are least effectively
fulfilling (10 of 10).

The importance of partnering with the parents and the home was pervasive throughout all the research. A few of their comments reveal how passionately leaders felt about the importance of the home and church working together to disciple kids:

> *"Success in children's ministry is connecting children and families to the Gospel. To bridge the gaps and provide parents with training and support to disciple their children."*

(Qualitative response to:
What success looks like in children's ministry)

(Quantitative response to:
Greatest challenges faced in children's ministry)

> *"The "busy" culture. In most families both parents work, their kids play multiple sports, and their schedules are packed. Parents are their child's greatest disciple maker. If the parents are too exhausted to come out to church, then their kids can't. If the parents are[n't] willing to help serve, then we sometimes struggle for volunteers. We can plan all we want, but if we can't awaken the parents to the importance of partnering with us to teach their child, it won't get very far."*

> *"Both the Leader and Parent Portals. I believe that these will be essential in keeping everyone involved. Real teaching begins at home, so this gets the parents involved and also keeps them accountable."*

(Qualitative response to: Specific features of a proposed children's ministry experience that stand out)

In Summary

A ministry resource or program that will meet these leaders where they live will help with the creation of better connections and greater impact between the church and the parent. There must be a shared set of values about the importance of the discipleship process with kids. There must be a shared passion that leads to real action and partnership between church and home. Just grabbing another program that does not share this value will fall short of what they need. Children's ministry leaders need help to facilitate community building with kids and families.

Questions for Children's Ministry Leaders and Volunteers:

1. Does your current curriculum or program help you awaken parents to their responsibility of disciple-making with their children?

2. Does your current curriculum or program give parents consistent next steps in becoming a disciple who makes disciples in their own home?

3. What words would you use to describe how your choice in curriculum or program engages parents or others in the home? How about your church at large?

6

We're Struggling to Develop Kids Who Can Navigate Culture and Live Out a Gospel-Centered Faith.

We're Struggling to Develop Kids Who Can Navigate Culture and Live Out a Gospel-Centered Faith.

Remember our friend Amy, the children's leader from the beginning of the book who talked about her kids being knocked over by the waves in the ocean? Amy's concern about being overwhelmed and even possibly overtaken by the rapidity and relentlessness of change is validated by the research. In the 2014 project, one of the ministry purposes tested relates to the impact of current culture on the kids they're trying to disciple.

"[The] greatest challenge is trying to teach and love children in a world that demands them to grow up too fast."

Developing Culturally Relevant Kids: Importance

Importance of developing kids who know
how to live for Christ in a postmodern age
(culturally relevant)

Total Respondents: 954

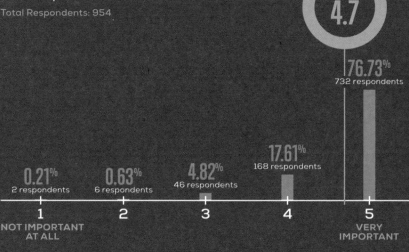

AVE. RATING:
4.7

76.73%
732 respondents

17.61%
168 respondents

4.82%
46 respondents

0.21%
2 respondents

0.63%
6 respondents

1 **2** **3** **4** **5**

NOT IMPORTANT
AT ALL

VERY
IMPORTANT

The attribute "Developing
kids who know how
to live for Christ in a
postmodern age (culturally
relevant)" was the third
most important ministry
purpose – only the Bible
and discipleship were rated
as more important. Most
leaders (94.34% 4+5 on
the 5-point scale) say
it is important or
very important.

To better understand this issue from the voice
of these leaders, here are a few of their word-
for-word comments to add insight to their
concerns about the impact of culture. When
asked to describe the greatest challenges faced
in children's ministry:

*"That they have so much exposure to the
mindset/worldview of American culture
and it infects the kids."*

(Quantitative response to:
Greatest challenges faced in children's ministry)

*"[The] greatest challenge is trying to teach
and love children in a world that demands
them to grow up too fast. Secular culture
is our biggest problem."*

(Quantitative response to:
Greatest challenges faced in children's ministry)

(Quantitative response to:
Greatest challenges faced in children's ministry)

*"Overcoming the culture and belief
systems that are so prevalent in a child's
everyday life."*

In addition, when asked what is the most important purpose of children's ministry, one answer that stood out pertaining to kids and penetrating the culture was the following:

> *"To equip kids to outreach in their own mission field that's all around them."*

(Quantitative response to: Most important purpose of children's ministry)

In Summary

Children's ministry leaders are concerned that the culture around their kids will overwhelm them and make them ineffective, ultimately causing their hearts to wander from God. They want a powerful ministry to kids that creates champions — young people who impact the culture and impact people for the cause of Christ and the Gospel. These children's ministry leaders are asking for their partners (those who provide resources, training, and programming) to help them equip and strengthen children to become countercultural spiritual influencers.

Questions for Children's Ministry Leaders and Volunteers:

1. Do you currently belong to a community of other children's ministry leaders and volunteers who are wrestling through this very same issue?

2. Do you know any churches tracking their effectiveness/progress in this area? How do they measure their progress?

3. Have you seen a track record or trend in your church ministry regarding kids who have grown up in your programs? Are these kids remaining and abiding in Christ as young adult disciples?

7

Children's Ministry Leaders Are Afraid We May Have Sacrificed Substance for Fun and Entertainment.

Children's Ministry Leaders Are Afraid We May Have Sacrificed Substance for Fun and Entertainment.

We've Got to Get Out of This Trap and Maximize Our Effectiveness.

There is no doubt the cultural shifts that are overwhelming families and ministry leaders has led to a shorter attention span and constant need to be entertained. The digital natives populating our churches and attending our ministry programs have been conditioned to experience the world on their terms and to move from one stimulating experience to another. They are rarely challenged or given space to think reflectively. In many cases, they easily become bored and distracted very quickly. Kids and leaders are all struggling through this reality.

Ministry leaders and workers have responded to this trend and the research we conducted bears it out. In their own self-assessment, children's ministry leaders say their ministry is unsurpassed at helping kids have an enjoyable experience when they come to church. They are having fun, but what's the trade off?

Nowhere is there a greater contrast in the research between what's important to these leaders and what they're doing well. **Of the 10 ministry purposes tested, Helping children enjoy their church experience – "have fun" is the least important (tied with Scripture memory).**

Having Fun: Importance

Importance of helping children enjoy their church experience – have fun

Total Respondents: 954

AVE. RATING:
3.82

0.31%
3 respondents

2.10%
20 respondents

13.10%
125 respondents

37.11%
354 respondents

47.38%
452 respondents

1   2   3   4   5

NOT IMPORTANT
AT ALL

VERY
IMPORTANT

By contrast, the churches these leaders serve meet this ministry purpose – having fun – more effectively than any other objective we tested. **It was number one in terms of what they do most effectively in children's ministry, yet they declared it to be of least importance in terms of making disciples.**

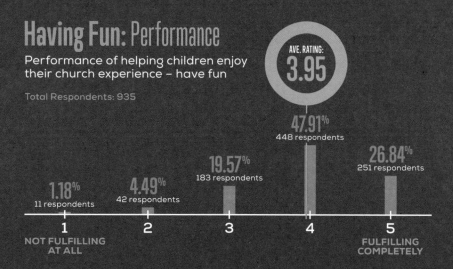

Having Fun: Performance

Performance of helping children enjoy their church experience – have fun

Total Respondents: 935

AVE. RATING:
3.95

1.18%
11 respondents

4.49%
42 respondents

19.57%
183 respondents

47.91%
448 respondents

26.84%
251 respondents

1   2   3   4   5

NOT FULFILLING
AT ALL

FULFILLING
COMPLETELY

On this point, research participants pointed the finger at themselves recognizing their priorities have gotten off-track. In their desire to be effective, sometimes children's ministry leaders have tried too hard to make their programming enjoyable and entertaining. Fun or style has unwittingly replaced substance and sometimes even sidelining the Gospel. From a few representative comments, a sense of frustration is rising and **there is a growing sense of resolve that something needs to change.**

"Big and fun is great to draw a crowd, but at some point we have to start influencing families to make good choices about their time."

(Qualitative response to:
Addressing real challenges in children's ministry)

(Quantitative response to: Why considering making a change in children's ministry programming in the next year)

"... we observed that the students lack Bible knowledge and were only interested in fun activities."

"Giving place to the Holy Spirit to do His work ... not getting so caught up in the "program" and the fun that we give no place for God to work."

(Quantitative response to:
Greatest challenges faced in children's ministry)

(Quantitative response to:
Greatest challenges faced in children's ministry)

"Children want to have fun ... but you have to teach the Gospel. A big challenge I face is combining the two. Teaching the Gospel so that way the kids can connect and still have fun. That they would enjoy learning about Jesus."

"I think more often than not children's ministry is more babysitting and fun than teaching children discipleship. How can we change this?"

(Qualitative response to:
Addressing potential new children's ministry resource)

In Summary

Children's ministry leaders we surveyed express concern that their approach may not produce the committed disciples they want. Entertaining programming is not enough. Honestly, churches aren't intended to compete with what the world is offering on this front. **Relevant disciple-making does not require a trade-off of the Gospel in favor of fun. Children's ministry leaders are asking for help in resetting their priorities; looking for ways to deliver substance so their programs are engaging but not focused too much on entertainment.** They'd like for kids to enjoy their church and children's ministry experience, yet they want them to grow in Christ and learn while they do. Any new programs or resources they will seriously consider must strike this balance.

Questions for Children's Ministry Leaders and Volunteers:

1. Do you believe the large group entertainment-driven discipleship model is on the front end of the innovation curve, or the back end? Is it effective? Why?

2. Does your children's ministry model major on entertainment yet produce little evidence of Gospel fruit in the lives of kids? How do you know either way?

3. Use your imagination, what would the perfect balance of style and substance look like? What would it achieve?

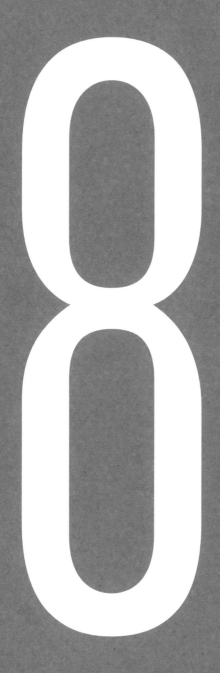

8

We Need a Program That Can
Meet Digital Natives Where They Are.

We Need a Program That Can Meet Digital Natives Where They Are.

One change that has made such a difference is technology. Children's ministry leaders recognize the need for children's ministry to meet digital natives where they are. The children and their families they are serving are immersed in all things digital. In increasing markets, kids and parents connect at home over mobile devices – whether they sit side-by-side to share or have access to their own screen. Getting and keeping the attention of kids (and some adults) is growing increasingly difficult and they need help.

"Many of our younger volunteers are also digital natives. I have very few volunteers that respond to email. They want me to tweet them ..."

One leader who participated in our focus groups was asked to describe the needs an ideal children's ministry program should meet, she said:

Others pointed out that the fact that this shift is happening and the language of technology is not just native to kids but also to young parents, and young adult volunteers in children's ministry.

"I would like to see digital follow up specifically geared to kids. They are always plugged in to electronics. What if Sunday and Wednesday lessons could be reviewed through online games. What if there was an Instagram-type page where they could enter photos and tell how they served others, or how they saw the lesson play out in their everyday lives that week. Parents would have a back door login to check their child's progress and answers."

(Qualitative response to:
What needs ideal program would meet)

"We are using more and more electronic media to minister. It's helpful because it is their "language." In fact, many of our younger volunteers are also digital natives. I have very few volunteers that respond to email. They want me to tweet them ..."

(Qualitative response to:
What needs ideal program would meet)

(Quantitative response to: Why you will consider making a change in your children's ministry programming in the next year)

"We are in a modern world and new technologies are helping to facilitate effective teaching and learning process that is why we are thinking of making a change."

These leaders summed up the perspective of many who are seeking innovative children's ministry programming and resources. These ideas were pervasive in the opinions captured in the research, especially related to new children's programming that might meet current needs. Further validation of this digital shift is found in the fact that more than one-half (55.89%) of the leaders we questioned prefer to receive their materials for children's ministry in a digital (downloadable) format. Many of these leaders, of various ages, have made this transition and prefer digital over hard copy. While digital-first and digital-only resources are still on the rise, digital access is a common need across current generations.

In Summary

To help with the problems children's ministry leaders are facing, they need approaches that will connect with and appeal to digital natives. These solutions need to be delivered digitally, should be intuitive for today's children and their parents, and should interact with the technologies they use every day.

Questions for Children's Ministry Leaders and Volunteers:

1. Do you prefer printed curriculum, some form of digital/downloadable, or a hybrid of both?

2. Do you see your need for digital/downloadable/mobile curriculum increasing in the future? For the kids, leaders, or both?

3. Does the thought of digital programming excite you? Scare you? Bore you? Why?

4. What opportunities for ministry does technology provide? What still can't be accomplished effectively through digital means?

9

We Need Flexibility So We Can Customize
to Our Purpose and Needs.

We Need Flexibility So We Can Customize to Our Purpose and Needs.

Change has highlighted the need for children's ministry leaders to adapt. In the 2013 research we conducted, when asked what was most important to them when they were looking for a children's ministry program, we learned that many leaders are looking for flexibility and adaptability of the program. We know they value, first and foremost, the Bible. But, the second most desired feature is flexible/adaptable/ease of use/creative. Many leaders think flexibility is the most important factor – their frustration with inflexible programs is obvious.

These leaders want a program they can customize to fit the challenges they face in their local ministries. They want a solid, trusted program that can be adapted to fit with their philosophy and vision as a church and as a children's ministry. Some representative comments help to clarify the ideas related to this value all in response to the question: "What would you say is the single most important decision-making factor when you are considering using a children's program or materials for your church?"

"Interested in the ease of preparation and flexibility for adaptation"

"Is the material Bible-based and can I adapt the material to my program?"

"Ease of use and adaptability"

"Easy to manipulate and mold to fit my environment"

"The flexibility and the amount of programming ideas; I like lots of options that can be fitted together."

"Is it easily adaptable to how we do ministry now? Prep and development time needed to make it work with excellence."

"Is the material Bible-based and can I adapt the material to my program?"

In Summary

"We need a flexible ministry resource" – this is what we heard from a number of leaders. Programs that are self-contained and inflexible are less effective. Plug-and-play made sense in the past, but now leaders need options that work in a variety of settings; resources that are flexible for a wide-range of group sizes, budgets, and priorities in churches.

Questions for Children's Ministry Leaders and Volunteers:

1. Does your current children's ministry curriculum align with your ministry philosophy; yet give you the desired flexibility you need to effectively make disciples?

2. Do you look for a turnkey solution or are you more interested in an adaptable curriculum?

3. Did you establish or inherit your current program and/or curriculum? What is keeping you or holding you back from making changes, if needed?

10

Children's Ministry Leaders Are Ready to Change If Curriculum Providers Can Serve Them With the Right Resource to Help.

Children's Ministry Leaders Are Ready to Change If Curriculum Providers Can Serve Them With the Right Resource to Help.

"We're thinking of making a change to help us be more effective at reaching kids" — this is what we heard from many leaders. All the changes and challenges confronted by children's ministry leaders leave them ready to consider their options. In the 2014 research, nearly one-half (46.66%) of these leaders say they are seriously considering a change in children's ministry programming in the next year. The leaders mention changing their curriculum/materials, more than any other factor. Nearly one-third (30%) say they would be most likely to change their curriculum/materials.

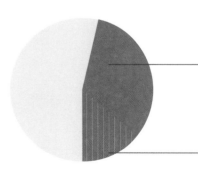

Are you seriously considering a change in your children's ministry programming in the next year?

46.66% = YES

Those of you considering a change, what would you be most likely to change?

30% = CURRICULUM/MATERIALS

Overall (or total sample) regardless of church size, denomination, or current children's ministry programming.

Many children's ministry leaders are open to considering other programs to meet the needs of the kids and families in their churches. **When asked why they were considering making a change, most said they just want to become more effective in reaching kids,** as clarified in some sample comments:

"Without changes, some of which are already being made, our church will become even more irrelevant than it already is."

"We are in a modern world and new technologies are helping to facilitate effective teaching and learning process that is why we are thinking of making a change."

"Looking for something that will grab the attention of the students to get them to realize that living a godly life is worth more than no godly life"

"I just feel like something is missing. I don't think our kids are getting as engaged as I would like them to and think they should be."

As children's ministry leaders, we need to be willing to be transparent about the self-reporting data. We owe it to the current and future generations to ask the hard and painful questions. This can be difficult when the findings suggest we need to make a change. But we believe the pain points are great enough, and that more and more children's ministry leaders are ready to make changes **to be more effective in stewarding the Gospel among children and their families.** The needs are clearer than ever and the culture isn't getting better. In fact, it is becoming more and more invasive. Rather than withdraw and retreat, we need to strengthen our kids in the Gospel — and our ministries with children and families — through a highly relational engagement and knowing God's Word.

It's apparent from all of our research that children's ministry leaders are ready for a new and innovative way to help produce lifelong followers of Christ while leveraging what matters most in discipleship (evangelism, relationships, and Bible teaching). We must pause, as the children's ministry community, and ask ourselves, "Are we simply running children's ministry programming? Or are we making disciples of kids, parents, and leaders?" We got into ministry because we wanted to reach kids with the Gospel and engage them as growing disciples ... not run complex, stressful programming ... or to babysit and entertain other people's kids ... or whatever lesser vision is taking over our core mission. How can we get back on track?

In Summary

Based on comprehensive research, Awana has identified the wants and needs that new programming should address. Over the last few years, as we have evaluated the research, studied the Scriptures, church, and culture, it's apparent that we need to reconsider a children's ministry model that's more effective in reaching and discipling kids. Even if it challenges us to change our current approaches or break out of the molds we have become so accustomed to, we believe it's worth it and we believe you do too. More than championing any single ministry method, we, at Awana, are more committed than ever to the mission of reaching kids all over the world with the Gospel and long-term discipleship. We are poised to impact this and future generations for Christ, but riding the wave of change is required.

The children's ministry community has spoken. The questions have been asked and the response has been heard. Over the years ahead, we anticipate more and more children's ministries adapting, innovating, and changing their models and programs in favor of laser-like focus on these key areas:

- Strong biblical foundation
- Centered on the Gospel and evangelism
- Focused on making disciples
- Highly relational
- Integration of church and home
- Appropriate leveraging of technology
- Flexible and adaptable programming support and curriculum

We must pause, as the children's ministry community, and ask ourselves, "Are we simply running children's ministry programming? Or are we making disciples of kids, parents, and leaders?" We got into ministry because we wanted to reach kids with the Gospel and engage them as growing disciples ...

For Amy and other leaders like her, Awana is available to partner with you in children's ministry. The waves around us need not sweep us away from our high calling to faithfully impact kids and families for the sake of Christ. We'd like to take some time to share how we can serve you and partner together to maximize effectiveness.

SUGGESTED SOLUTIONS

One Mission. Many Methods.

Awana graciously recognizes that we are one of **many** trusted ministry partners with an effective track record of Gospel-based ministry. Our commitment to discipleship that is both highly relational and highly biblical can be seen in our 65-year legacy in partnering with churches and families globally to effectively cultivate growing disciples. In the pages that follow, we invite you to consider how we can serve you and your church as you minister to reach and disciple this generation and the generations to come.

The GREAT Life Curriculum

The GREAT Life Curriculum

After two years of research and listening to those who lead children's ministry in the local church, Awana is proud to present its newest offering, The GREAT Life™. **The GREAT Life is a relational discipleship curriculum** for kids ages 5-11. It leverages interaction with Guides, parents, and peers to lead kids along their spiritual journey. Built on the idea of having a group of kids (suggested max of 12) and two adults in a GREAT Life Circle, kids will be guided through the Old Testament in Year 1 and the New Testament in Year 2. Each GREAT Life Circle Time and accompanying GREAT Life Family Experience leads kids to see Christ in each story as they are moved to know Christ, love Christ, and serve Christ, together.

The curriculum is developed to include a GREAT Life Family Experience which is done prior to coming to The GREAT Life Circle. The GREAT Life Circle Time is led by two adults who, during their preparation, have been challenged to reflect upon and apply the content to their own discipleship walk. Adaptable for use in a 60-90 minute time frame, it can be done anytime and anywhere, and is **perfect for Sunday morning!**

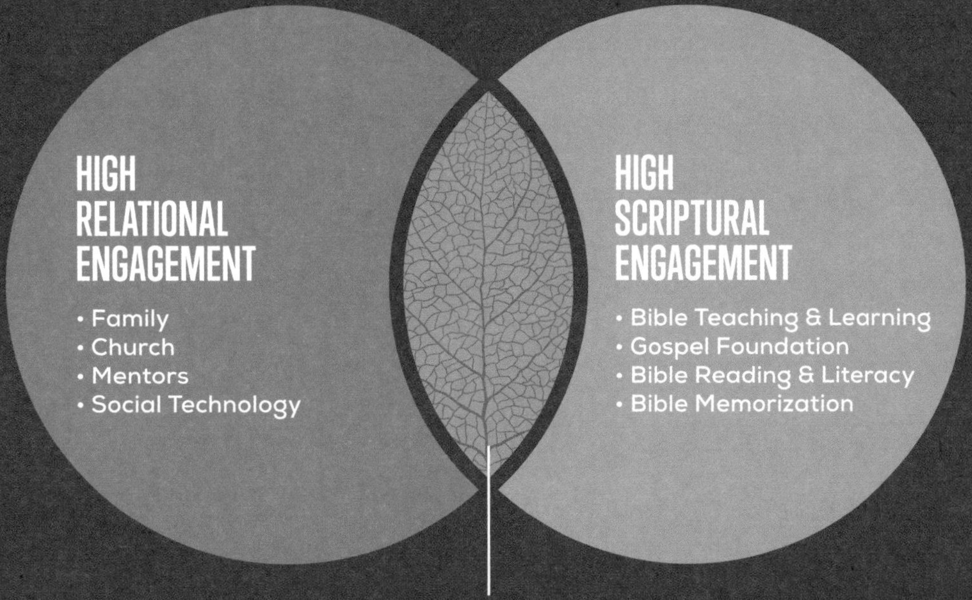

HIGH
RELATIONAL
ENGAGEMENT

• Family
• Church
• Mentors
• Social Technology

HIGH
SCRIPTURAL
ENGAGEMENT

• Bible Teaching & Learning
• Gospel Foundation
• Bible Reading & Literacy
• Bible Memorization

The GREAT Connection
is the sweet spot of discipleship.

The GREAT Connection Is the Secret Ingredient.

What sets The GREAT Life apart from other children's ministry offerings is the combination of scriptural engagement and relationship, the leveraging of technology, and engagement of Scripture. Awana has always followed a Relational Discipleship Model seen throughout Scripture and church history that has been all but forsaken in the modern age of turnkey curriculums and checkbox Christianity.

Through The GREAT Life, children will be given a solid foundation for lifelong discipleship and guided forward on their spiritual journey as they are captivated by knowing Jesus Christ, consumed with loving Him and compelled to serve Christ and others. This is achieved through the rich and relevant study of God's Word, guided discussions, reflection with the group, and opportunities to serve.

Why The GREAT Life?

The GREAT Life is so named as it reflects the challenge to all of us as Christ's disciples to embrace and experience "Four Great Goals." These great goals include:

- **The Great Calling** of following and knowing Jesus Christ.
- **The Great Commandment** of loving Jesus and loving others.
- **The Great Commission** of serving Jesus and serving others.
- **The Great Community** of gathering in unity in the Body of Christ.

The Bible Is Our Constant Source of Truth.

Awana has always placed a high emphasis on biblical literacy and the difference that can be made through intentional relationships between adult leaders and kids in the Awana program. Beyond these church relationships, The GREAT Life equips churches to build and fortify great church-parent partnerships in order to create a more effective and authentic discipleship model for kids.

We Will Always Make Disciples.

As a ministry focused on the evangelism and discipleship of children and youth, Awana is excited to introduce you and your ministry to The GREAT Life. Your volunteers will grow in their depth of faith as they engage with the materials in order to lead the hearts and lives of children through encountering the Bible and allowing the text to transform and shape them. The GREAT Life leverages technology, relationships, and Scripture to provide an engaging and life-changing discipleship experience.

The **GREAT Life curriculum will launch Fall 2016** and be available in a customizable digital format for use on a mobile device or printed for hard copy use.

The great life is life in Christ, the life Jesus has called His followers to live. If you want to see your students go from simply learning about the Bible to being transformed by the Scriptures, check out The GREAT Life. Find out more about how The GREAT Life can equip your church and enrich your Sunday morning experience at **awana.org/thegreatlife**.

2

Flexible Awana Club

Flexible Awana Club

For years, the general consensus among the children's ministry community has been that the church gets one of the 168 hours in a child's week. That understanding has made popular the phrase, "Make Sunday the best hour of a child's week."

The trouble with that understanding is, that it assumes a child shows up **every** week.

A new challenge issued in *The Question Nobody Asks About Our Children*, by Larry Fowler, challenges churches to take a closer look at their attendance for the purpose of finding out how often each child actually attends.

Based on case studies, Larry realistically found that children's ministry leaders **aren't** getting one hour of a child's week. **Instead they're lucky to get 25 hours of a child's whole year!**

So what's a children's ministry leader to do?

Larry offers numerous suggestions in his book, but the very first is to reconsider a midweek program for kids. By simply creating more opportunities for discipleship and by running programs throughout the week (when schedules are more stable) there is a dramatic rise in consistent attendance.

For 65 years, kids from pre-school to high school have engaged in a holistic discipleship experience all wrapped in relationship through Awana midweek programs. Awana reaches kids and connects them to trained, equipped leaders for proven long-term discipleship.

Awana alumni are

3.6

times more likely
to read their Bible several times a week

NEARLY
70%

said they witness to
their friends at least
once a month

92%

still attend church weekly or more often

Consistent, long-term participation in Awana – between 6-10 years – accompanied by spiritual training from parents, reaps long-lasting results.

customizing. The mission of Awana is simple; to reach more children with the Gospel and help them become lifelong followers of Christ. **That mission is unwavering, but our methodology is highly adaptable.**

"Being someone who has been involved in children's ministry, I find myself awake at night thinking about the kids who are walking away from their faith once they get into adult life…[It] became personal to me when I heard some of the kids that attend our own church that actually chose that path."

This pushed Pat Cimo, Director of Family Life at Willow Creek Community Church, to begin searching for answers and solutions to help move a child further in their spiritual journey. That's when she discovered Awana.

Pat learned that Awana was flexible and customizable to the culture at Willow Creek, and it became a great solution for their discipleship ministry.

One Size Does *Not* Fit All.

Over 65 years of ministry provides a lot of time to make changes and learn to adapt. In recent years, adapting the traditional club model has become an priority for the ministry. **Awana has made a commitment to putting Gospel mission over ministry method.**

Awana will work in any Bible-believing church, club, or community program with a little

See the whole story of Willow Creek's discovery process and the results of their decision to use Awana at **awana.org/willowcreek**.

While you're there, take advantage of a special offer to **try 30 days of Awana completely FREE**! A whole month of our curriculum is available for download at **awana.org/30daysfree**.

3

Mozo Technology

Turn Minutes Into Ministry With Mozo.

Awana has long been known for its unapologetic declaration of the Gospel, high Scripture engagement, and an emphasis on biblical literacy. What few may recognize, however, is that since Awana Co-Founder Art Rorheim first began the ministry in 1950, every element of the program has been wrapped in relationship with God and each other.

The time between a child and leader, discussing God's Word, or simply talking about all that makes up a child's daily highs and lows, is intentional and can hold eternal significance. Those moments and conversations represent an investment on behalf of the leaders to cultivate a relationship where they have earned the right to speak, teach, and model scriptural truth for the children they lead. **Relationships are the secret to success behind the Awana discipleship program.**

Awana believes the only way to grow children into lifelong disciples is to utilize these intentional relationships. It is within the context of these relationships, and upon the foundation of scriptural knowledge received in Awana, that children are equipped to successfully navigate our ever-changing culture that can often be contrary to biblical truth.

While this relational discipleship model is intended to be the bedrock of the Awana program and is the desire of children's ministry leaders of all kinds, the business of ministry too often fills the time necessary for this level of intentionality. Processes, unexpected events, miscommunication, scheduling, and hundreds of other tasks make cultivating those intentional relationships a challenge. We need to leverage available technologies to help us be more effective at solving these challenges. The time is now, which is exactly why we have developed the Mozo™ Digital Platform.

The business of ministry too often fills the time necessary for this level of intentionality.

* The screen images shown here are representative of the Mozo 1.0 menus and interface. Actual and current screen images and icons may differ from those shown here.

Introducing Mozo Technology

Mozo is a digital tool for Awana ministries that was built to make recordkeeping, award tracking, attendance, communication, team collaboration, and leadership development as efficient and as simple as possible. All done for the purpose of freeing up more time for relational discipleship. No more flipping through stacks of paper or binders to track a child's progress through the program. No more frustration at the rounds of communication needed with a KidMin team or lack of communication due to inefficient communication channels. No more excuses for being ill-prepared or under-resourced when it comes to leadership training and development. Now all of that can be accomplished on a smartphone, tablet, or on a computer; through the simply, easy-to-use, mobile-friendly interface of Mozo, a web-based program.

Take care of administrative tasks quickly so you can spend your time where it matters most.

*

Tracking kids' handbook progress is simple.

Automate your award lists and tracking.

Take attendance quickly.

Keep volunteers on the same page with the shared club calendar.

Collaboration is easy with centralized messaging.

Access full library of club resources – Large Group lessons, games, training, and quick tips.

It is the hope of Awana that Mozo will make being a leader a little easier, and free leaders up to spend their time where it matters most. No one was inspired to become a children's ministry leader because she loved the paperwork, all day training sessions, or endless rounds of emails and group texts. Children's ministry leaders chose to invest their time because they want to see more kids come to know, love, and serve Jesus for a lifetime. Mozo was built so that Awana leaders can spend more time focusing on that kind of life change, and less worrying about the process that facilitates the program.

* The screen image shown here is representative of the Mozo 1.0 menus and interface. Actual and current screen images and icons may differ from those shown here.

Turn more minutes into meaningful ministry with Mozo. For an up close look and to add Mozo to your ministry toolbox visit awana.org/mozo.

APPENDIX

The 2013 Research Project – Raw Materials for New Development

Research Purpose

In January of 2013 the leadership team at Awana sensed the need to "take the pulse" of the children's ministry community. With a strong sense that major shifts were happening, the Awana team made a significant commitment to a research study. The objectives of the project were clear. In addition to assessing the programs of Awana, **the desire was to fully understand the wants, needs, and expectations of children's ministry decision makers.**

Specifically Awana wanted:

- To identify the critical factors children's ministry leaders value when choosing a children's ministry program provider for their church.

- To understand how children's ministry leaders are influenced to make choices about their program providers.

- To identify sources of information for children's ministry products and programming used by children's ministry leaders.

- Generally, what is most important as these leaders make programming and partnership decisions.

Methodology (Combined Qualitative and Quantitative)

The 2013 project used a combined methodology which began with in-depth interviews with church children's ministry leaders and Awana missionaries. A total of 41 of these 25-30 minute interviews set the stage for the quantitative phase which involved two audiences, the first of which was Awana employees. From the in-depth interviews and the employee survey (with 165 total participants), much was learned that has contributed to the ongoing developments at Awana.

The Children's Ministry Marketplace Survey

The critical learnings in the 2013 project came as a result of the study entitled *The Children's Ministry Leader's Survey*. The 376 completed surveys of children's ministry decision makers nationwide were extremely valuable in terms of what was learned. Much of what has been reported in *The Gospel Truth About Children's Ministry* was learned in this phase of the research. The highly statistically-valid study (+– 5.05% margin of error) helped set the direction for the development of The GREAT Life presented in this writing.

Research-Aided Development

This study quantified the opinions of children's ministry leaders and revealed some of their wants and needs that, for the most part have been unmet. These findings were one of the motivators that compelled the team at Awana to develop a new approach to children's ministry. Having listened to the children's ministry community and heard what they viewed as important (even vital) new ministry resources were conceived. These bold initiatives and innovations developed after the 2013 research were taking shape and as the team moved closer to implementation, the leadership team once again decided research was necessary for confirmation.

SURVEY #1

376
COMPLETED SURVEYS
(SAMPLE SIZE)

±5.05%
MARGIN OF ERROR

The 2014 Research Project – Confirmation That Awana Was "On the Right Track."

Research Purpose

Once again the leadership team saw the need to conduct research. This time the decision was driven by the desire to reconfirm the direction, gleaned from the 2013 research, which had driven new program development. In addition, the Awana team needed to confirm that there was a willingness in the marketplace to switch to new programming if it addressed the needs so clearly expressed in the previous study.

Specifically, the study purpose was:

- To test (confirm/disconfirm) the basic ideas and marketplace needs on which The GREAT Life is based.

- To explore features and program elements of The GREAT Life to see if they meet the current needs.

- To test the ideas about delivery and technology.

- To sharpen the resources based on feedback from respondents.

- To understand the desire in the community for change.

Methodology (Quantitative Followed by Qualitative)

It was determined for the 2014 research that a combined methodology was also the most appropriate approach. However, the sequence was reversed. The desire was to first confirm or disconfirm the basic ideas that had driven the development of The GREAT Life children's ministry resources. After confirming that these new and innovative ideas were on target overall, the qualitative phase could be used to explore the specific features and components to gain in-depth feedback from these leaders.

Children's Ministry Marketplace Survey 2 (Substantial Response)

Once again in 2014, a comprehensive study was distributed nationwide. A total of 858 children's ministry decision makers completed the full survey. This large response yielded a highly statistically-valid response (+-3.35% margin of error). **With high confidence, Awana leaders were able to say the ideas were overwhelmingly confirmed.** The survey focused more on the purpose of children's ministry and the outcomes these leaders viewed as a success. This is in contrast to assessment of the features and components of children's ministry programming – much of the 2013 focus. The priorities used to develop The GREAT Life foundation and structure were overwhelmingly aligned with the results of the quantitative research (much of which is reported in *The Gospel Truth About Children's Ministry*).

SURVEY #2

858
COMPLETED SURVEYS
(SAMPLE SIZE)

±3.35%
MARGIN OF ERROR

Online Focus Groups
(In-Depth Assessment of Ideas)

Some of the 858 respondents who completed the quantitative survey were recruited to participate in online focus groups. In those focus groups they were presented with the details of the new proposed programming and were asked to provide their in-depth ideas about these components. The desire of Awana was to further confirm that not only was the overall direction of the new resource aligned with needs, but the specifics of the execution were as well. Three online groups of 20+ respondents each were conducted over a three-day period. The discussion guide allowed for great flexibility and probing to investigate every aspect of these leaders' opinions. The ideas of these groups added insights and, once again, confirmed the direction and details of The GREAT Life resources.

Awana leaders' claim that they have "listened to children's ministry leaders," is based on having made an extraordinary effort to gather valid research findings from this population using an excellent sampling source. Awana conducted extensive primary research in the children's ministry market over a period of two years. The direction and details of The GREAT Life programming is based to a great degree on listening to and responding to a representative sample of children's ministry decision makers across the country.

About the Authors

Matt Markins

Matt serves on the Global Leadership Team at Awana as the Vice President of Ministry Resources as well as the Vice President of Marketing and Strategy. Prior to joining Awana, Matt served in leadership roles with Thomas Nelson Publishers, Randall House Publishers, and was the co-founder of the D6 Conference (a discipleship and family ministry community). He and his wife Katie have been volunteering and growing in children's ministry for more than 20 years. They live in the Chicago suburbs with their two sons tolerating dreadful winters, but soaking up amazingly mild weather the other seven months of the year.

Dan Lovaglia

Dan is the Director of New Ministries and Parent Engagement at Awana. He is the co-author of *The Gospel Truth About Children's Ministry* (Awana, July 2015) and *Relational Children's Ministry* (Zondervan, Spring 2016). The team he leads is finding fresh ways to equip kids, families, and ministry leaders to know, love, and serve Christ. Dan and his wife Kate live in the northwest suburbs of Chicago with their two fantastic teenage sons, Avery and Aaron. Follow his adventures on Twitter and Instagram: @DanLovaglia.

Mark McPeak

For nearly 25 years, Mark has specialized in helping companies and organizations with major strategic decisions. Meeting with senior leaders and identifying key questions, Mark helps define the market intelligence needed to move forward. Once the data is collected and analyzed, Mark provides strategic recommendations and works with the client team to maximize results. Mark is the founder and president of Sightline Research + Strategies.